AFFIRMATIONS TO OVERCOME ANXIETY

MICHELLE MANN

Copyright © 2021 by Michelle Mann

Affirmations to Overcome Anxiety

All rights reserved.
No part of this publication may be reproduced, distributed, or transmitted in any form or by any means, including photocopying, recording, or other electronic or mechanical methods, without the prior written permission of the publisher, except in the case of brief quotations embodied in critical reviews and certain other noncommercial uses permitted by copyright law.

Although the author and publisher have made every effort to ensure that the information in this book was correct at press time, the author and publisher do not assume and hereby disclaim any liability to any party for any loss, damage, or disruption caused by errors or omissions, whether such errors or omissions result from negligence, accident, or any other cause.

Cover design: Ajao Ifeoluwa
Formatting: Ajao Ifeoluwa

First Edition 2021

Contents

If you have an anxious mind	4
Begin with the following calming statements	5
Your outlook on everyday life	6
When you worry about decisions that you made	8
What is your motivation for getting up in the morning?	10
Worry has no space in your place	11
Anxiety comes from the unknown	12
Speak the opposite to yourself	13
Goal setting, a way to overcome anxiety	14
They may offer relief when nothing else does	45

If you have an anxious mind...

If you have an anxious mind, it is sometimes a difficult task to settle your mind and relax. With these daily affirmations, you will be able to overcome the anxiety and become calm in the middle of the storm.

Start your day by speaking these affirmations to yourself while looking in the mirror. Looking yourself in the eye while speaking these life-affirming statements will build your self-confidence and reduce your anxiety.

Begin with the following calming statements..

1. I am calm.
2. I have survived my worst days and better days are ahead.
3. There is beauty within me that is reflected around me.
4. Today, I will say no to negative self-talk!
5. There is power in how I react to the people around me.
6. If I do not give them the reaction they are expecting, their actions will change.

Your outlook on everyday life..

Your outlook on life determines the colors of the rainbow that you see in your life. If you only see gloom and doom and dark and dreary days ahead, you will miss out on the days that are filled with bright beauty because you are focused on only the darkness.

7. What happened yesterday has no control over today.
8. The future is bright and filled with new blessings that are waiting for me.
9. What looks bad to me now will turn out for the best for me.

10. Obstacles are just stepping stones to something better.
11. I am overpowering stress. Stress cannot overpower me.
12. I have the ability to change my mind.
13. I am valuable. I make decisions that give value to myself.
14. I make decisions to compose my life story.
15. I can make an entrance everywhere I go.
16. I am serene. I will not panic.
17. I am in control of my emotions.
18. I can shake off these anxious feelings.
19. I am smiling.
20. I will laugh and not panic.
21. I will pay attention to the thoughts that I think. I will change the thoughts that are causing me to be afraid.

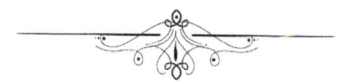

When you worry about decisions that you made...

When you worry about the decisions that you made because your information has changed about the situation, and armed with new information, you would have done things differently, use these affirmations to get rid of the negativity.

22. I made the best decisions I could make with the information that I had at the time.
23. I will make the best decisions I can make with the information that I have today.
24. I will be kind to myself as I am kind to others.
25. Nothing I face today will be more than I can handle.
26. Emotions are like the wind, and anxiety has blown away.
27. I can learn something new today.

28. I touch my nose. I touch my toes. Anxiety has to go!
29. Worry is the logical expectation of feared things to happen.
Calm is the logical expectation of wonderful things to happen. I choose calm.
30. Anxiety has an ending point. It ends right now!
31. I have positive reactions to every situation.
32. I am not running in the Anxiety Marathon. I have retired those sneakers, and I have on my happy dancing shoes.

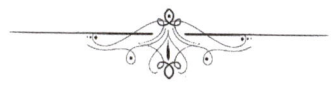

What is your motivation for getting up in the morning?

What is your motivation for getting up in the morning? Is it dread or excitement? If you are dreading the day ahead, you will only want to pull the covers tighter over your head and avoid the new day. If you are excited about the new opportunities that the new day brings, you will bounce out of bed with a glow that will excite those around you. Use these affirmations to kindle the glow in your life.

33. I am motivated to enjoy every single day of my life.
34. I will smile at a stranger today.
35. I am giving myself gratitude every day.
36. I am here to impact my corner of the world.
37. My smile is the meteor that blasts out anxiety.
38. I will see the best in every situation.
39. I can retrain my brain to hope instead of worry.
40. I am shifting the gears of my attitude to hope.

Worry has no space in your place..

Worry has no space in your place. Worry has a negative voice that you will learn to recognize. When you hear Worry speak, talk back and scare Worry away with these affirmations.

41. Worry has no place in my space.
42. I can boss Worry around!
43. I can outsmart Worry's tricks.
44. I refuse to play with What If today.
45. I am talking back to Worry today.
46. I am not going to listen to Worry anymore.
47. I am not surprised that Worry showed up today, but Worry can go now.
48. I am not confused by Worry today. I can do this.
49. I am taking control of my life back from Worry.
50. I am breathing out all of the Worry's germs in me today.

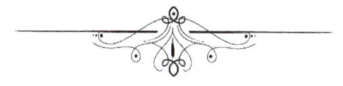

Anxiety comes from the unknown...

Anxiety comes from the unknown. If you are prepared to experience the unknown, anxiety has no power over you. Putting yourself in uncomfortable situations can create practice situations that prepare you to overcome anxiety by remembering your successes during practice. Like with anything else, practice makes you better at it than you were the day before.

51. I am a little nervous, but I won't be for long.
52. I am practicing being uncomfortable today. I am going to win today.
53. I am willing to feel unsure and will embrace not knowing what will happen next.
54. I am willing to try something new without expecting to be an expert right away.
55. I am able to trust myself to do something new.

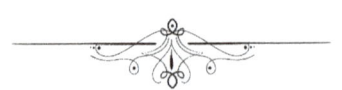

...Speak the opposite to yourself...

Trade-in what the negative voices in your head are telling you for the opposite message. When worry tells you that you should be afraid, speak the opposite to yourself. You can have courage in new situations.

56. I am going to experience new things today.
57. I am courageous.
58. I am looking forward to today because good things will find me today.
59. I can handle feeling nervous and doing it anyway.
60. I remember being scared the last time I tried something new. I can do something new again.
61. I can tolerate making a mistake today.

Goal setting...a way to overcome anxiety ...

Goal setting is a powerful way to overcome anxiety. When you are focused on achieving a goal and working daily to make sure that you achieve it, you won't have time to let anything else cross your mind.

62. I am going to reach the goal I set.
63. I am going to follow my dreams.
64. I am training myself to be successful.
65. I will only compare myself to measure how much better I will be tomorrow.
66. Everything I will do today will be one step toward a better future.
67. I am going to do my best in all things today.
68. I am going to leave behind old insecurities today.
69. I am going to put my best foot forward in every situation today.
70. I am an empowered person. I control my reaction to the situations I face today.
71. I face this day with enthusiasm instead of dread.

72. I start this day with an optimistic outlook. There is no Negative Nelly here.
73. I set my mind to face my fears head-on and power on through them.
74. I am able to identify negative thoughts and cut them off at the pass.
75. I am proud of my ability to control my thoughts and emotions.
76. I am able to soothe myself with deep breaths.
77. I am able to remember a happy place and smile.
78. I am able to slowly count to ten and focus my thoughts. I can be at peace instead of anxious any where that I am.
79. I am not afraid.

80. I am caring for myself first today.
81. I believe in myself and my abilities.
82. I will be content today with who I am.
83. I am going to finish one task at a time today. I do not have to be worried about my to-do list today.
84. I am important to myself. What I think about my self matters more than anything else.
85. I am able to choose to be calm today no matter what happens.
86. Even if today is tough, tomorrow is a new chance to start over.
87. I will pat myself on the back today for even the small victories.
88. I am safe and peace surrounds me.

89. I am owning my feelings. They are real, but they are able to change.
90. I am owning my thoughts. They are mine, but I can change them.
91. I can say no without an explanation. It is my right.
92. I can say yes to doing things for myself without feeling anxious about saying no to others.
93. I know I am doing my best.
94. I am able to turn stress into motivation.
95. I trust myself to make good decisions even when I don't know exactly what will happen next.
96. I am friendly and can enjoy meeting new people.
97. I am parking my worries at the door today.

98. I am stronger than my fears are telling me that am.
99. I am scared, but I don't have to stay scared. I have courage.
100. I may struggle today, but I will overcome.
101. I am able to ask for help when I need it. Asking for help is not a sign of weakness.
102. I will conquer today's fears, and they will be be hind me tomorrow.
103. I am learning that I am an overcomer.
104. I can choose what I think about today.
105. I am responsible for my happiness and no one else's.
106. I am letting go of anxiety.

107. I am proud of what I did yesterday and what I will do today.
108. I give myself permission to be anxious for 15 minutes. After that, I will be calm and relaxed.
109. I am glad that I focus only on what I can do today.
110. I am less anxious today than yesterday.
111. My mind is made up. I will not fear.
112. I forgive myself for being afraid of the unknown.
113. I am a social butterfly and will make the rounds through the room without fear.
114. I am able to make eye contact with new people while we talk.
115. I am comfortable in a crowded room.
116. I am graceful and thoughtful toward others in a social setting.

117. I can put people at ease when they are feeling awkward.
118. I am able to speak well with others.
119. I like making conversation with people I don't know very well.
120. I am as important as everyone else. We are all the same size under the stars.
121. I am loving life and all of the hope of tomorrow.
122. I am focused on the goal ahead. I won't stop now for fear!
123. I am covered in calmness.
124. I remember how anxiety feels, and it can go now.

125. I am aware of my surroundings. I am safe and sound here.
126. I have my life skills toolkit. I am prepared for anything life throws at me.
127. I am able to walk in and stand tall today.
128. I am able to speak clearly and get my point across without stammering.
129. I am able to show kindness to those who are unkind to me.
130. I am able to do more than others think I can.
131. I am able to sail through life's storms. My umbrella boat is made of my smile.

132. I am going to succeed in what I have set my mind to do. Fear is just a stepping stone to something better.
133. I am going to sing my way through the struggle.
134. My home is my fortress, and I am safe here.
135. I am creating my own safe haven from the stress outside.
136. I am creating my own future one day at a time.
137. I will not fail me.
138. I will provide for myself.
139. I will love me today and always.
140. I will give myself time to rest today.
141. I will sing a new song today.
142. I will power through the scary parts!
143. Once this is behind me, the easy stuff is next!

144. I am comfortable with who I am today.
145. I am confident that today will be better than yesterday.
146. I am wiser today than yesterday.
147. I am going to change what I can change today.
148. I am absolutely worth doing my best today.
149. I will listen before I speak.
150. I am thankful for the opportunity to do new things today.
151. I will honor myself today with a treat for defeating fear.
152. I choose to forget yesterday and focus on today.
153. I am persistent and fear must take a back seat to day.
154. Today I will start something new.

155. Today I will be thankful for everything.
156. I see the beauty in tackling new things.
157. I am thankful for the lesson life taught me in how to overcome.
158. Good things are worth working for.
159. Today is just one day in this phase.
160. Seasons come and go. Today is the start of a new season.
161. I am giving myself kudos for doing my best.
162. I am a very strong person even when I don't realize it.

163. I am energized instead of anxious.
164. I am looking for happiness today.
165. The best parts of my life are under construction today.
166. I am trading the gloom and doom clouds for sun shine today.
167. I can have joy today. It is within reach.
168. My joy doesn't depend on anyone else.
169. My happiness is mine, and I fiercely protect it.
170. My magnetic personality only attracts happy people.
171. I am willing to find happiness today instead of fear.
172. I will use the struggle of anxiety to polish my smile.
173. Confidence is blooming in me today.
174. I will catapult forward from the setbacks of yesterday.

175. What happened last time won't happen again.
176. I am determined to smile instead of fear.
177. I am grateful to be alive.
178. I hop over obstacles to get to my goal.
179. I owe it to myself to be happy today.
180. I am confident and fearless today.
181. I am courageous today.
182. I am a life transformer.
183. I am believing that I can do what needs to be done.
184. I am proud to be who I am.
185. I am motivated to win.

186. I am excited to find out what the future holds.
187. I am embracing change instead of fearing it.
188. I am okay with making mistakes because it means I am learning something new.
189. I am confident enough to try something new and risk not doing well at first to have a new experience.

190. I send the pain of yesterday to forgetfulness.
191. I am empowered to face all of my fears head-on.
192. I will face one fear today and overcome it.
193. I will do better today than yesterday because I learned from my mistakes.
194. I have unlimited ability to learn.
195. I have unlimited ability to laugh at fear.
196. I will willingly take a chance today without knowing the outcome.
197. I will try a new restaurant by myself and not wonder what people think.
198. My struggle will help someone else overcome.
199. I am on pace to reach my goal ahead of schedule.
200. Anything that looks like a setback is just a setup for success.
201. I will see the good in myself.

202. I will praise myself when I do something scary today.
203. I will give myself grace instead of judgment.
204. I will release myself from fear today.

205. I am excited about what is coming next in my life.
206. I trust that I will take care of myself in any situation.
207. I am powerful in the moment that seems scary.
208. I am trading overwhelming fear for courage.
209. I will pull out all the stops to overcome what I am afraid of.
210. I understand what I am afraid of, and I can conquer it.
211. Instead of negative outcomes, I am focusing on the positives.
212. Instead of worrying about what might happen badly, I am imagining the good things that could happen.
213. My mind is my own, and it is clear from fear.
214. I will replace the fear statements with a victory song.

215. I can choose to look for the good instead of the bad.
216. I am choosing peace instead of turmoil.
217. I will make good choices for myself today.
218. I am opening myself to good possibilities.
219. I am glad that I can step into new situations.
220. I can carve my own niche in life without fear.
221. I have a clear vision of what I want to happen.
222. I will trust that what I do will be the right thing for me.

223. I am relaxed in my own skin.
224. I am stronger than the fear that is trying to scare me.
225. I have a vision for my life that energizes me.
226. I have a plan and will follow through.
227. I am choosing to do the next right step.
228. My vision is becoming reality.
229. My potential is blossoming into reality.
230. I will sit and breathe when I feel afraid.
231. I trust myself to survive again.
232. I am focused on one idea at a time.
233. I am bringing my dreams to life.
234. I am working toward a better life.
235. I am training myself to be an overcomer.

236. I am training myself to run the race without fear.
237. I can see the light at the end of the tunnel.
238. I can think thoughts that empower me.
239. I can see the victory ahead.
240. I set myself free from the guilt of yesterday.
241. I am away from danger.
242. I am loved and respected.
243. I am secure in who I am and the choices that I make.
244. I can identify anxiety and put a stop to it.
245. I can identify fear of failure and recount my successes.
246. I am stronger than the feelings of fear tell me that I am.

247. I am well and able to overcome doubt.
248. I am useful and can help others overcome fear.
249. I have people that I can lean on for support.
250. I can do it alone, but I don't have to if I don't want to.
251. I am a leader and can show others the way to success.
252. I refuse to let this get me down! Anxiety is a feeling and nothing's wrong with feeling feelings.
253. I am committed to being my best and the most genuine version of myself.
254. I can do anything if I take a deep breath first and feel good inside my skin.
255. All these fears have been so unimportant, they're just in my head.

256. The wind is blowing through me and everything else that has tried to stop me has failed.
257. No matter where I am, I'm always going to find a way back here--to the present moment as it is really happening now.
258. You don't need to be perfect. You will make mis takes while doing your best, which is all anyone can ever ask for.
259. When I'm discouraged or anxious, I remember that it's temporary and will eventually pass making room for peace because silence always follows an argument.

260. Life presents so many opportunities; there are things in my life that I have the opportunity to work on and take part in so why should anxiety dominate it?
261. Life has too much to offer for us to escape from the stage through worry any longer-life is happening right now waiting for us to join in on the adventures!!
262. I have the power to stop my thoughts and then I can relax.

263. I'm capable of being happy because happiness comes from within and not from any external sources.
264. When I release all these feelings, they won't c ontrol me anymore. It's easier said than done, but with practice, it will get better.
265. I am an all-powerful person. I can do anything I set my mind to if I believe in myself.
266. This is why it's important for me to take care of myself-- so that I don't just go flying into an abyss of panic, worry, and questions that have no answer.
267. I choose to be brave and proud of who I am. My anxiety doesn't define me but it's always a part of me.
268. Sitting with my thoughts is so hard, but now I've found the courage to live for today by trusting in

tomorrow.
269. My worries fall off as they get tired and bored trying to keep up with my living life on purpose.
270. It's okay to feel anxiety.
271. Self-development is worth a little discomfort! I am comfortable being uncomfortable because people need me for all the positive changes they're going through when they're opening themselves up to self-development more than ever before!

272. If you don't keep moving forward nothing will change--so get back up and live with purpose even if that means anything goes wrong along the way!
273. I'm able to take in all the beauty and love in my world. I am more and more able to let go of anger, pain, regret, or anxiety so that it can pass from me as though any emotion is just a passing guest.
274. Love life no matter what! I love my inner beauty.
275. I am full of joy because each day is precious, a gift!
276. Living in peace and harmony with all that is around me at this very moment.
277. Let today be better than yesterday--then reset tomorrow to automatically make it even better.
278. I have the power to stop my thoughts and then I can relax.
279. Start by committing to something that makes you feel good every day

280. I'm still finding the courage to live for today by trusting in tomorrow, but with that in mind, I can handle any challenge.

281. Today I'll be proud of myself because I dealt with one of my fears and overcame it while my anxiety dissipates.
282. I forgive myself when I make a mistake, and that m akes me more self-confident to move on with life.
283. Today is the day I will find happiness and joy by living fully and doing what's best for me.
284. The only 'reason' for anxiety is because it hides something even better than you or your current situation.
285. I'm a happy-go-lucky person. I can feel the joy in life, yet not worry when things don't go as planned.
286. Nothing will stop me from living this amazing and beautiful life!

287. My resilience is growing daily! I look forward to my newfound power!
288. My anxiety eases because it takes one breath at a time to be present with all the love that surrounds me every day.
289. Mountains of peace and joy rise in my being, bringing me closer to the best version of myself.
290. I have been given the gift of life on this Earth--so let me make the most of it.

291. My worries slip away as I shift my focus to what brings me simplicity and joy.
292. Today, I take steps that lead to a brighter tomorrow, leaving behind any guilt or shame.
293. No matter what happens today, I will always be able to live in peace with myself.
294. I can worry less and focus more on the good things to come.
295. I am a happy person, who can sometimes feel anxious because it means that I care about myself.
296. Anxiety is normal for everyone because we all have doubts and fears now and then. It's simply telling me what I need to work on in my life at this moment.

297. My anxiety is just a signal from unknown territory--I know there are solutions waiting ahead because I've already overcome so much!
298. I can handle any challenge that life throws my way.
299. My anxiety is nothing more than the anticipation and fear of change.
300. Many times, I'm anxious when I'm not even solving a problem at all! And so, what is there to be anxious about?
301. Every day leads to an even better tomorrow.
302. I can do hard things. I am genuinely happy and have a well-rounded life.
303. I will not live in fear because I am not a victim.

304. Did I beat my anxiety today? You betcha!
305. There is much joy ahead of me, and that's what life is all about.
306. Nothing stands in my way of taking charge of my life! My new sense of purpose gives such great relief from any fears about tomorrow!
307. I am very strong. Nothing can destroy me because I am stronger than my anxiety!
308. I will do what is best for me and trust myself be cause the right choice always reveals itself in time.
309. I love and accept myself.
310. When my anxiety makes me feel less worthy or not good enough, I remind myself that nothing could be further from the truth.

311. Today I choose to find strength for every obstacle through deep breathes and grounding poses. So be with me.
312. I now realize that anxiety is just a way of showing up for something better in my life.
313. My heart is full and soon, it will overflow with joy.
314. Anxiety is accepting this positive change as I transition into the new person I am meant to be.
315. I keep forgetting that I am the only one who's fully responsible for my own happiness.
316. Life is good when I focus on what is in front of me

with gratitude and self-worth.
317. I am strong enough to handle my problems be cause I can take care of myself.
318. I'm resilient! I have the strength to endure any challenge.
319. I am self-reliant. When it feels like I'm drowning, my true abilities are revealed.
320. I love myself unconditionally and believe in myself 100%

321. I am proud of myself!
322. Anxiety is telling me that I'm sensitive to my environment, and that gives me room for growth.
323. A wonderful life is waiting for me ahead. The only thing standing in my way is what makes this excitement even better--my anxiety!
324. Refrain from dwelling on the past or fighting feelings of anxiety with worry and fear.
325. I am always moving, and I will not be hindered in my goals.
326. I love life just the way it is. Every day brings new opportunities!
327. Exercise. Move your body in a way that feels good. Sometimes it's all you need!
328. I'm a leader, not a follower. I'm confident in my skills and abilities to make an impact on the world.
329. I take care of myself by being honest about what I want and need; this means I don't have to guess or second guess myself anymore!

330. Anxiety is just trying to hold me back from living out my true potential--my life's goal isn't to be paralyzed with fear, it's letting go of the things that don't matter when there's so much more waiting ahead!
331. I am strong.
332. When I'm anxious, I remind myself that the past is irrelevant and worry about what might happen in the future because it's inevitable no matter who I am.
333. Anxiety builds my confidence because I know that nobody can feel worse than me when it comes to being anxious.

334. I am at peace.
335. I am strong, capable, and worth it. I deserve to feel good about myself too.
336. We will overcome anxiety by accepting the fearful thoughts, but not giving in.
337. Every day it becomes easier to cultivate peace, love, and positivity around us. We have learned to live without fear over time. It is beautiful the way our bodies react because we are powerful beings filled with curiosity about life and challenge!
338. Anxiety cannot stop my inner strength from shining brightly!
339. I am resilient! I have the strength to endure any challenge.

340. I am self-reliant, and when things feel like they are getting too tough, it always reveals my true skills.
341. I CAN get things done at work – and I will.
342. I'm beautiful, inside and out.
343. I am clever and intelligent. I have many skills that are needed in the workplace, so I must be valuable!
344. I am an asset to my company!
345. I can show my worries to someone I trust, and they will help me work through them.
346. I have friends or family who are on my side.
347. My anxiety is not a problem that needs fixing because it's just the natural result of caring about myself--though it might be hard sometimes, I still deserve kindness too!

348. Every day is new and brings progress I may never see at first sight.
349. Being anxious doesn't make me broken but reminds me of how much strength to grow in and understanding what life wants from me.
350. Some days aren't okay, but most days are good enough for me.
351. Not every mantra or piece of advice will apply to me, and that's okay. There's nothing wrong with that! Besides, I have many other solutions at my fingertips!

352. I am strong and resilient. I have so much to offer the world--and those around me.
353. Everything is for my own good! Every little thing, in all its unfolding of life's purposes, is there because it will make me a better person - it was meant just for me!
354. My anxiety or fear never has anything to do with what I can't handle. It only tells me that this challenge is trying to teach something important about myself: how much more self-compassion and patience I need to have if these challenges are going to be faced head-on!
355. It feels great when I create space for peace in my mind by changing my attitude and doing something kinder instead of making excuses or judging others harshly.

356. I have the power to make my mood!
357. Yes, I can chill out and take time for myself every now and then.
358. I now pause to just be. I am here and in the moment with myself.
359. I am who I choose to be. My fearlessness will lead me to success every single time, as long as I'm willing to work for it.
360. Some days are rough but that doesn't matter because this day is going great so far!
361. Today I tell anxiety "Enough!" It's up to me now

how today feels.
362. I realize that anxiety is temporary. It doesn't have to take up permanent residence in my life and lay waste to it.
363. I can change the way I feel now by using some coping skills for anxiety. As simple as breathing, repeating a mantra, or taking an actionable step, I can ease myself out of any anxious thoughts or feelings.
364. Believe that there are solutions in every moment, just waiting to be found.
365. I can do something about it and rise up from past failures, knowing I am the same person despite the change.
366. It's just a feeling that I can choose whether or not to validate by reflecting on my life moments-- nothing more.

367. My anxiety means that there is something to progress within my life. Just noticing where to improve shows how strong I am already!
368. Anxiety will not stop me because it only makes me hesitant to take action or make changes for fear of what might happen if things go wrong. But never mind - because it doesn't have any power over me as I take one step at a time!
369. Work on the steps I need to take to continue progressing, ignoring my anxious thoughts when

370. I am never alone because something good always comes from discomfort and challenges.
371. I'm in the process of recovering from my anxiety. It's okay to be where I am today.
372. I can ask for help and recognize that it's much easier when I work with others instead of doing it alone.
373. I can't wait to be intimately acquainted with my femininity.
374. Life has taken care of me well, and I can let go of worrying about things that don't serve my best interests.
375. I have so much to offer the world--and those around me.

376. I can do things that seem almost impossible some times, just because I know I have the support of my friends or family when the going gets tough. And my anxiety will be there too!
377. All my stress is based on a lack of self-worth or ability; but in reality, it has no right over me and needs to be put in its place!
378. Every negative feeling is a gift of learning more about myself--my inner self, not what others think I should be like.
379. Even if it feels heavy to carry responsibility around every day, I can't give up because it's the start of

what I want to change!

380. I'm more worthy now than I've ever been. Today starts a new day where nothing is decided, and that also means everything is possible.
381. You are strong beyond belief. You can do anything that you put your mind to, and life is going to be good!
382. Thankful for the opportunity and adventure which lies ahead of me!
383. It's not a waste of time if I take care of myself first. Anxiety comes and goes, but it always does--oh, the relief!
384. I can live in the moment, breathe deep and enjoy the present hour.
385. I am enough right now, and this moment is all I need to start feeling better.

386. I surround myself with the things that make me happy, even if it's as simple as a walk outside.
387. You are more than OK, and life is good!
388. Affirming my worth, I know that I deserve anything good which comes my way.
389. Sometimes I want to hide under the covers and never come out, but then I remember that there are so many fascinating things in this world for me to experience.
390. Life is worth living. There is always something beautiful around life's corner.

391. I'm the best person for myself!
392. My body is a vehicle for my spirit, and my spirit renders me invincible.
393. I am constantly evolving into more than I thought it was possible to be.
394. I'm more worthy now than I've ever been.
395. Today starts a new day where nothing is decided, and that also means everything is possible.
396. Today will be an adventure in learning more about myself.
397. Talking to people is always a good option when it feels like anxiety is getting to me.
398. I'm better than my worst enemy, and they can't stop me from doing the things that are important to me.

399. I am not afraid to be comfortable in my own skin.
400. Life's too short for inaction--start that new business!
401. I know I can't get everything done at once, but it feels good to try!
402. All the pain I don't run from today is just energy for a brighter tomorrow.
403. I am at ease. I relax and allow my body to breathe in its natural state.
404. I was born with a lot of potential, and I haven't lived up to what's possible for me; so today is the

day where that stops!
405. Good things are waiting for me when I'm ready to embrace them--and I've reached this point because hiding hasn't worked either.
406. I have no rules and I am excited to say that's okay!
407. I have the power to control my feelings and any change in them!

408. One day at a time!
409. I am what I am, and I love who I am!
410. Eat right, sleep well; exercise, and laugh every day.
411. Anxiety, you can't break me!
412. No one is in charge of my life but me!
413. My anxiety is a gift from my body reminding me to appreciate it more.
414. I have a right and obligation to do what feels best for me--nothing more.
415. It's my tough times that make the good times so wonderful.
416. The feeling of being scared or overwhelmed doesn't have power over me to make mental predictions about today meaning disaster because all it does is tell you how much work you need to do on yourself before looking outside again!
417. Allowing time for reflection and feeling, I quiet my mind.
418. I trust myself. I am a magnificent person, worthy of all the best things in life.

419. I choose to look at this situation differently! Nothing is set in stone, so if something isn't working right now moment-to-moment it doesn't have to define me or define how I move forward for the rest of time.
420. My anxiety might be trying to scare me off from taking risks which are good for me--but no more looking back!

421. I am love, and so are you.
422. The future is not set--let's see what we make of it!
423. Everyone deserves to have a voice and be able to speak their truth.
424. Today is a day of growth and refinement.
425. I am taking back control over my emotions, and that's okay.
426. I nurture my worries now--rather than running away from them.
427. I don't need to take life so seriously.
428. I am going to stop and make my presence felt in the world today.
429. Loving myself is the most powerful way to keep a clear, grounded perspective.
430. I am the observer of my thoughts and feelings--not their slave.
431. As I reflect and allow myself to feel, this negative emotion passes like the stormy clouds in a sky clearing up!

432. I trust myself.
433. If things aren't going your way now moment--to-moment, then they won't define you as a person forever - all things are impermanent, and fleeting--no one thing defines you for the rest of time.
434. This stress will only last until tomorrow! So, let's see what we'll make out of it and not judge ourselves too harshly.
435. We deserve more than this wordless suffering--give yourself some love!
436. The future is not set; there is still hope! --let's see what we accomplish together.

437. Everyone deserves forgiveness and happiness even though sometimes circumstances don't seem fair.
438. Today starts with me forgiving my worries rather than running away from them unto others.
439. I trust myself. I am a magnificent person, worthy of all the best things in life.
440. I am now, and always will be, in the center of my life.
441. I allow myself to feel right now, without judgment or condemnation.
442. I know that what hasn't happened yet is not a measure of who I am.
443. I am a powerful person.
444. I take care of myself every day--doing what I know

is good for me emotionally, and physically.
445. It's alright to feel scared, but that's not the end of the story for me. It couldn't be!
446. I am giving myself credit for something I've done or felt--and that's okay. A great thing, even!
447. I choose to let go of judgment and perfecting.
448. I refuse to let my mental health dictate how I am going to live the rest of my life.
449. Now that you've built yourself up, it's time to also believe in yourself.
450. I work with what I know rather than how I feel.
451. I have the power to choose how my day goes.

452. I deserve to be loved.
453. I am worthy of my life, and I receive it.
454. I love myself for who I am.
455. I refuse to be overwhelmed by my thoughts and emotions.
456. I am taking back control of my life--choosing a new way forward.
457. It's okay to feel what I'm feeling, and it doesn't mean anything is set in stone.
458. Worrying too much keeps me from focusing on the present moment, which might be just fine!
459. I have the power to be at peace, even in my most stressful times.
460. Confidence is something you do not need to worry about; it just shines through you--and I've always

got that on standby!

461. I deserve peace and happiness on a daily basis.
462. Today, I am going to make three conscious choices.
463. I will use my voice and speak up for myself
464. Mindfulness is all about being free from judgment--so don't judge yourself. You are awesome.
465. I am going to focus on the present and live in this moment, effectively coping with my anxiety.
466. It's okay if I feel uncomfortable--this means I'm taking risks!
467. The more comfortable I get, the less my anxiety will try to control me.
468. The future is not set, and I am going to stop looking ahead. I am important and this moment matters. Giving myself some space will help me feel grounded again.

469. I don't need to be perfect to feel good about myself. I love and accept myself just as I am!
470. With every moment, the future becomes clearer and more illuminated by our loving presence.
471. I'm not going to be stopped from achieving my goals because of my anxiety.
472. I have a lot of things which I don't need to worry about!
473. I am going to trust myself and do what I know is good for me tomorrow.

Affirmations to Overcome Anxiety

474. I am learning the key to living with anxiety: not taking life so seriously--and intending with humor always.
475. I am allowing myself to feel, without judgment or condemnation.
476. I love myself.
477. I am strong enough to experience every aspect of my life.
478. My thoughts and feelings are just a filter--not an actual portrayal of truth.
479. I choose to soften instead of harden, and learn from adversity rather than resisting it.

480. My thoughts are not the boss of me! We'll work together--not against me.
481. What my anxiety wants is for me to feel uncomfortable or powerless--but I don't have to.
482. I accept the things I cannot change, and then take action to make an impact on those I can.
483. The world needs me!
484. I am going to take a break from my expectations of myself.
485. If left unchecked, this anxiety will only get worse and bigger and more serious--I know what I need to do!
486. Today feels good.
487. Mental health is just as important as physical health--guess I'm getting on that right away!
488. I don't need to be perfect to feel good about myself.

I love and accept myself just as I am!

488. With every moment, the future becomes clearer and more illuminated by our loving presence.

490. I'm not going to be stopped from achieving my goals because of my anxiety.

491. This might make me nervous, but I'm going to do what's best for me.

492. At this very moment, I breathe easily and deeply! At this very moment, all is well.

493. It doesn't matter how bad it is--it can only get better! It will be a great day today!

494. My thoughts and feelings are neither good nor bad, they just ARE.

495. As the anxiety builds, I ground myself in my soul.

496. I am strong enough to experience every aspect of my life.

497. I accept that it's OK to feel anxious. I am not withdrawing from life, but facing it head-on.

498. Good things are happening for me as a result of my efforts!

499. I am unstoppable.

500. Today was hard, but tomorrow will be better because I am in charge of my life.

501. It's going to take a lot of practice and work for me to feel like anxiety is a positive force in my life, but that's alright--I want that!

... They may offer relief when nothing else does ...

Affirmations have always been a major part of dealing with stressful situations and are one of the most crucial tools you can use. They may offer relief when nothing else does, no matter how anxious one might be feeling. It is important to make sure that the affirmation is said using a positive tone for it to be most effective. Many people find the best use for affirmations when used not only during moments of anxiety but also as a routine part of your day and then they can go back to them daily and get better over time by constant practice which will allow them to calm down easier than before. One thing should be remembered though; affirmations are not magic, rather, they work due to purposeful, long-term practice of positive thinking in which you become receptive to change and learn to implement change independently using these tools.

You may notice one day, after weeks of practice, a change in your thoughts from negative ones about yourself or the world around you, into realistic statements that are full of self-acceptance and understanding. Acceptance of all of your accomplishments, all of your faults, and all of your potential – so that you can conquer your anxiety so long as you have enough perseverance. You may see yourself in a better light, have a better mood, become more motivated, be more effective at problem-solving, and with a better sense of optimism. Affirmations have been shown to activate the brain's reward system, which softens the blow of physical and emotional stress and decreases the perception of pain. In other words – it is real, and it's scientific!

This is all possible for you, as long as you persevere and maintain a realistic mindset. Affirmations work best for those who choose to affirm themselves with statements that are realistic for them personally. Otherwise, you may become discouraged, feel incapable, and unsuccessful, when simply the chosen affirmation was the wrong fit for your personal needs.

For an extra powerful transformation with affirmations, feel free to make some of your own as well. You can make your own with a notebook and pen before bedtime by writing down one thing that came up the day that made you feel anxious. Write it as though if someone else had said it to you and what they would have said next (a suggestion) so you write it for yourself. Use this as a goodnight note each time something aggravating comes up and let the rest of them pile on there so they're always accessible when ready to use whichever affirmation applies currently. As mentioned, be sure to keep your affirmations personally believable and realistic. Personalize your affirmations by keeping them in the first person ("I", "me", "my"). Keeping your affirmations in the present tense instills a sense of realism. It feels more real, and more possible, if it's now and not in the future. If you state them to yourself as if they're already true, it can be far more motivating. Accept your anxious thoughts so that you may practice self-love and take them head-on, if you can face them, you can affirm yourself out of them. And, while you're at it with self-love – tie your affirmations to your core values and successes, so that you may nurture yourself and have compassion for yourself. Tying affirmations to core values is very grounding, makes them real, and easier to remember in stressful moments.

Affirmations are highly helpful and effective for many people, but for some, they are not the end-all, be-all of managing anxiety. (And that's okay!) If you find that your anxiety is severe and persistent, overwhelmingly affecting daily functioning, relationships, work, school, or physical health, it may be time to consult with a doctor or therapist to guide you through your recovery. Sometimes, it's as simple as a health issue causing the anxiety (such as hyperthyroidism) or bringing in a professional who can help identify your triggers and methods that work for you. Many people do, and there's nothing wrong with needing or asking for help. It doesn't mean that your affirmations aren't good enough, or that you're doing anything wrong.

And now, I have an affirmation for YOU – when you use these tools, you will be replacing your anxiety with realistic statements that highlight your full potential, and over time it will become easy to move on, simply LIVE, and conquer stress!

CPSIA information can be obtained
at www.ICGtesting.com
Printed in the USA
BVHW012335290523
665041BV00019B/451